.

better together[*]

*This book is best read together, grownup and kid.

 akidsco.com

a
kids
book
about

a kids book about CHRONIC PAIN

by Cherie Kroh

a
kids
book
about

A Kids Book About, Kids Are Ready, and the colophon
'a' are trademarks of A Kids Book About, Inc.

Printed in the United States of America.

A Kids Book About books are available online: *akidsco.com*

To share your stories, ask questions, or inquire about bulk
purchases (schools, libraries, and nonprofits), please use
the following email address: *hello@akidsco.com*

Print ISBN: 978-1-958825-33-4
Ebook ISBN: 978-1-958825-34-1

Designed by Rick DeLucco
Edited by Emma Wolf

For those in chronic pain—I believe you.

For those 4 important people in my life
who believe me—thank you.

Intro

As grownups, we often believe that we can successfully hide aspects of our lives from our kids, especially in the hopes of protecting them when they are young. I learned very quickly that there isn't much kids don't pick up on. They are aware, sensitive, and inquisitive little humans.

Living with chronic pain and all that comes with it is not worth hiding from your kids. I worried that if they knew about my chronic pain, it would make them feel sad and uneasy. But it turns out, they were already feeling those emotions; they just didn't know exactly why.

My hope is that this book helps you start the conversation for any kid with a grownup in their life who lives with chronic pain. Through understanding, we build connection. And who better to focus on building that connection with than the kids in our lives?

When you wake up in the morning, what are the first things you think about?

For me, the first question on my mind is, **"HOW BAD WILL MY PAIN BE TODAY?"**

THAT'S BECAUSE I LIVE

WITH CHRONIC PAIN.

What is chronic pain?

The word "chronic" means "continuing or repeating."

SO, CHRONIC PAIN DOESN'T EVER STOP OR FULLY GO AWAY.

When you scrape your knee or hit your funny bone, those aren't examples of chronic pain (though they do really hurt in the moment!).

Chronic pain is a physical condition that can occur anywhere in the body and impacts everything you do and how you feel.

With each new day, I have to focus my mindset and make plans based on how strong the pain is for that day.

THAT USUALLY MEANS CHANGING MY PLANS.

For example, my partner and I walk our dogs together. But on my hardest days, he needs to walk them on his own.

I need to adjust the way I work and how I spend time with my kids.

How I prepare meals is based on my pain too.

I even plan what I'll wear each day based on my pain level. (High heels aren't my friend!)

And I'm not the only one who deals with my chronic pain on a daily basis.

My family does too.

DOES THAT SOUND FAMILIAR TO YOU?

Do you have a family member with chronic pain as well?

My kids and partner have learned to be flexible with their plans. Sometimes, plans change, and that can be disappointing.

But my family is so supportive.

THEY HELP GET ME

When I first started experiencing chronic pain, I wanted my kids to know that I was going to be OK.

My older son was worried my condition was contagious and was curious if he would get it too.

My younger son wanted to know if I would die because of my chronic pain.

The answer to both is no.

THERE ARE MANY CAUSES OF CHRONIC PAIN.

BUT THERE IS NO ONE SOLUTION OR CURE.

My chronic pain is in my low back. It feels sharp and lasts all day long.

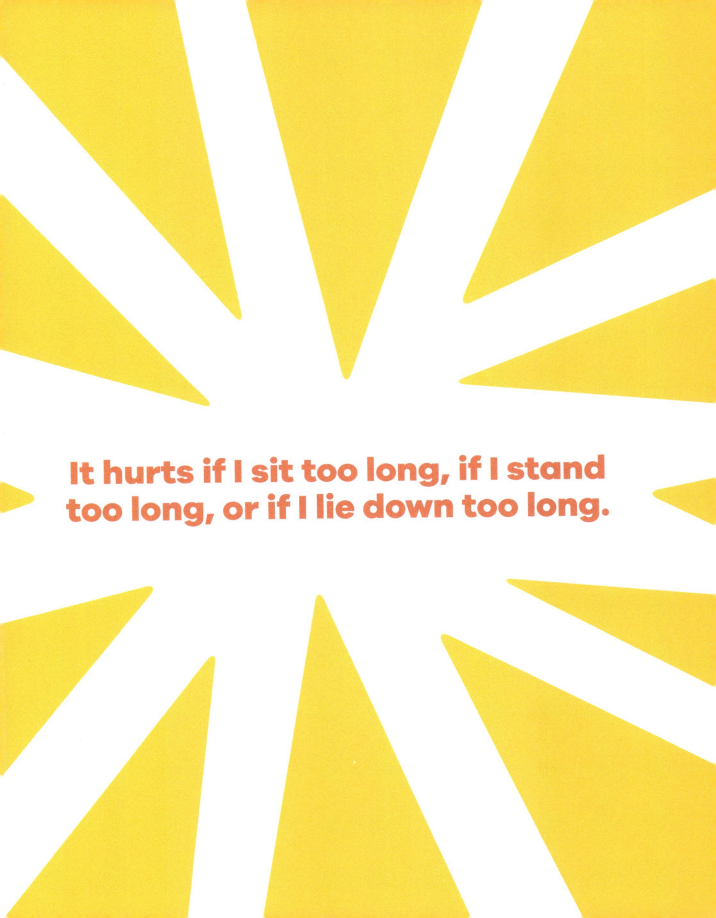

It hurts if I sit too long, if I stand too long, or if I lie down too long.

Chronic pain can come from injuries, accidents, and diseases like cancer or arthritis.
But the pain is not contagious.

So if you know someone who lives with chronic pain, don't be afraid to give them hugs and love them up close. I know the attention means so much to me!

AND JUST BECAUSE CHRONIC PAIN CAN HURT A WHOLE LOT,

IT DOESN'T MEAN SOMEONE WILL DIE BECAUSE OF IT.

I know it's scary for my kids when I have to spend a whole day in bed. **But my body needs that to feel better on hard days.**

And if I don't take that time to rest, it gets worse. I end up with more days where I can't spend time with my kids.

For those of us with chronic pain, we all manage it in different ways. I've tried many things and found what works best for me.

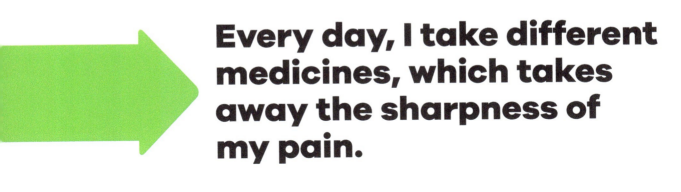

Every day, I take different medicines, which takes away the sharpness of my pain.

I use ice packs to help me stay focused at work, where I usually sit or stand for a long time.

I also take a bath every night. I haven't missed a bath in 8 years!

By the end of the day, my pain is too bad to stand in the shower. Also, taking a bath helps me fall asleep.

Other things that help people with chronic pain include changing how you focus on your pain in the first place, meditation, and mindfulness, like taking time every day to practice gratitude.

It's so important to spend time thinking about what's good. Otherwise, you'll just be overwhelmed by what hurts.

And that doesn't mean you can't feel sad or frustrated. Having chronic pain is so hard!

**One of the worst parts
is sometimes feeling like
I'm missing out on fun things.**

For example, my kids love jumping on trampolines. They laugh and have so much fun!

But that's not something my body allows me to do. So I've found other ways to connect with them.

We go to movies,
work on art projects,
and roast marshmallows
in the backyard.

My older son is great at solving the Rubik's Cube, which I can do with him (even though I still haven't solved one)!

You may be wondering if there's anything you can do to prevent chronic pain from happening in your body.

And I'll tell you something really interesting!

One of the things
that can prevent chronic pain
that can prevent chronic pain
is the same activity that helps
people manage their chronic pain:

MOvE

MENT.

You're probably thinking, **"WHAT?!"**
I know that sounds backward!

**When you move your body,
your brain releases chemicals*
that makes your pain feel better.**

*Those chemicals are called endocannabinoids.

Simply taking my dogs for a walk helps me get through the toughest part of my day.

Movement helps your joints stay lubricated and keeps your muscles warm and flexible!

It also gives you more energy and helps you clear your head. Movement makes you feel good!

Having chronic pain isn't fair. It isn't fair to the person who has it or their loved ones.

But please know this:

THE PERSON IN YOUR LIFE WITH CHRONIC PAIN IS SO GRATEFUL FOR YOUR FLEXIBILITY AND SUPPORT WHEN THINGS HAVE TO CHANGE.

When I am having a bad day, my kids take on extra chores.

They don't argue with me when there's something I can't do, and they come up with things for us to do together, even if they'd rather do something else.

They're not happy about it all the time! But they love me, and that's more important.

We work together to get to a place where we can find predictability in unpredictability.

I AM A PERSON WHO HAS CHRONIC PAIN, BUT IT ISN'T EVERYTHING I AM.

I AM
A MOM,
A TEACHER,
A PARTNER,
AND I LOVE
THE PEOPLE
IN MY LIFE.

My good days are always really good days.

And when I need to rest, I know my family is there for me.

THAT WAY, I CAN BE THERE FOR THEM TOMORROW.

Outro

So, where do we go from here? Keeping the conversation going and remaining open to all questions that may come is key. Through discussion, you might explore:

- Ways in which grownups can communicate their increased pain on a given day

- How stress, emotions, and even how we think about pain can alter how pain feels

- Ideas of how to help the grownups in their life with chronic pain

- How to learn more about chronic pain, advances in science, and those who experience chronic pain

As grownups with chronic pain, we don't want to burden our kids with the daily realities of it. But I want to encourage you to let them in. When you do so, and when the time comes for them to deal with any pain, physical or emotional, they will let you in. And that is the whole point.

About The Author

Dr. Cherie Kroh is a "guide on the side" to 2 very inspirational and understanding humans, Canyon and Myosin. She lives with her partner, who is an exceptional coach with a presence that makes every day better. They all live in Salt Lake City, Utah, where the mountains call each day.

She is the owner and CEO of Wellness Coaching Elevated and Director of Integrative Health and Wellbeing Coaching at the University of Minnesota. She is a former dancer and runner, and is an advocate for health coaching in healthcare and physical activity for enjoyment, healing, and mental health.

She does not know what causes her chronic pain, but will never lose hope in scientists searching for all the answers.

 @inclusivehealthcoaching   @coachingelevated   @cheriekroh

a kids book about MONEY by Stramwasser

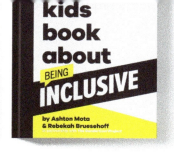
a kids book about BEING INCLUSIVE by Ashton Mota & Rebekah Bruesehoff

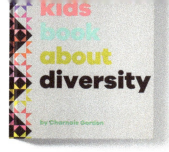
a kids book about diversity by Charnaie Gordon

a kids book about LEADERSHIP by Orion Jean

a kids book about IM... by M.

a kids book about SAFETY by Soraya Sutherlin, CEM in partnership with JUSY

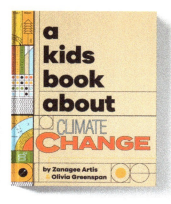
a kids book about CLIMATE CHANGE by Zanagee Artis & Olivia Greenspan

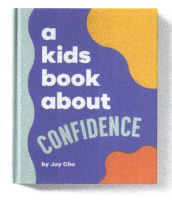
a kids book about IMAGINATION by LEVAR BURTON

a kids book about CONFIDENCE by Joy Cho

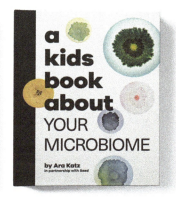
a kids book about ANXIETY by Zabo Happy Faces

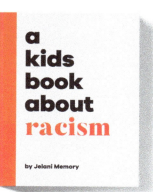
a kids book about YOUR MICROBIOME by Ara Katz in partnership with Seed

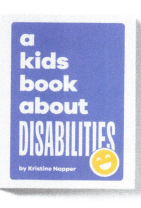
a kids book about racism by Jelani Memory

a kids book about DISABILITIES by Kristine Napper

a kb ab ab by: Ky

a kids book about DIVORCE by Ashley Simpo

a kids book about cancer by Dr. Kelsie Storm & Sarah Porter

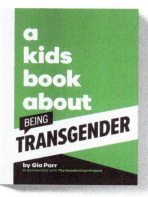
a kids book about BEING TRANSGENDER by Gia Parr in partnership with The GenderCool Project

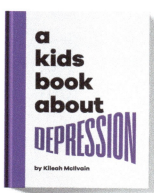
a kids book about DEPRESSION by Kileah McIlvain

a kids book about Shame

a kids book about THE TULSA

Printed in the USA
CPSIA information can be obtained
at www.ICGtesting.com
LVHW070942171023
760424LV00018B/87

9 781958 825334